LIFE

Growing

By Holly Duhig

BookLife
PUBLISHING

©2019
**BookLife Publishing
King's Lynn
Norfolk PE30 4LS**

All rights reserved.
Printed in Malaysia.

A catalogue record for this
book is available from the
British Library.

ISBN: 978-1-78637-442-4

Written by:
Holly Duhig

Edited by:
John Wood

Designed by:
Jasmine Pointer

Photocredits:
Images are courtesy of Shutterstock.com. With thanks to Getty Images, Thinkstock Photo and iStockphoto.

Front cover – all_about_people. 2 – tankist276. 3 – all_about_people. 4 – Andrey_Kuzmin, Valentina Razumova, cynoclub, Olga Sapegina, Chepko Danil Vitalevich. 5 – Kevin Eng. 6 – blessings, iko, Subbotina Anna, tmcphotos, April_pie, 9george. 7 – Steven Hogg, plavevski. 8 – Sergey Uryadnikov. 9 – John Carnemolla. 10 – Cheryl E. Davis. 11 – Tatyana Greenlees. 12 – Zykov_Vladimir. 13 – Jarabogu. 14 – 22August. 15 - Sakdinon Kadchiangsaen. 16 – Awei. 17 – Steve Byland, SIMON SHIM. 18 – Anatolich. 19 – Althea Gianera, Matthias Brix. 20 – Bogdan Wankowicz. 21 – Studio 37. 22 – Monkey Business Images. 23 – Africa Studio.

Contents

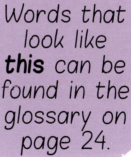

Words that look like **this** can be found in the glossary on page 24.

What Is a Living Thing?

A living thing is something that is 'alive'. Humans are living things; so are cats, dogs, birds and fish. There are certain **processes** that make something a living thing. These are:

Growing

Eating

Reproducing

Getting Rid of Waste

Breathing

Some things,
such as metal,
plastic and rocks,
have never been
alive.

Some things used to be alive but are now dead. The bones you give your dog, the brown leaves in autumn, and the wood that makes your furniture were all parts of living things that are now dead.

What Is Growing?

Humans grow a lot!

Growing is the process that all living things go through when they change and get bigger. Some living things grow and change a lot, whereas other living things don't grow much at all.

When giraffes are born they are already one-tenth of the size of their mothers. However, the babies of giant pandas are tiny when they are born. They have a lot of growing still to do!

Newborn Panda

Mammals

Mammals give birth to live **young** who they feed with milk from their bodies. Baby mammals usually look like their parents when they are born, but much smaller.

Elephant babies look like smaller versions of their mothers.

Kangaroos are a type of marsupial but they are also mammals. Kangaroos never stop growing!

Mammals will usually grow very fast when they are young and stop growing once they have reached adulthood. However, some mammals keep growing until they die.

Birds

Birds start life as eggs. Once they have hatched they are called hatchlings. Hatchlings are smaller than their parents and they don't have any feathers. They need their mothers to keep them warm.

Once the hatchling has developed soft feathers and grown a bit bigger, it is called a fledgling. A fledgling's feathers will fall out and be replaced with stronger feathers when it becomes an adult.

Fledgling

Fish

Most fish start their lives as eggs. When they hatch, they are called **larvae**. Larvae are still attached to the yolk sac of their egg. Yolk sacs give the larvae the **nutrients** they need to grow big and strong.

Yolk Sac

Once the larvae have used up all the nutrients in their yolk sacs, they have to start looking for food themselves. At this stage, the fish are called fry.

Reptiles

Most reptiles will shed their skin many times before they are fully grown.

Reptiles have skin made of scales. As they grow bigger, their skin doesn't grow with them. This means they have to shed their old skin and grow a new one underneath. This is called moulting.

Some reptiles shed their skin in patches. Others, such as some snakes, shed all their skin at once. Young snakes shed their skin every few weeks because they are growing quickly.

Adult snakes usually shed their skin two to four times a year.

Snake Skin

Amphibians

Tadpoles

Amphibians are creatures that spend some of their lives in water and some on land. Frogs are amphibious. They start their lives as tadpoles living in ponds. They have **gills** and tails so they can live and breathe underwater.

Small frogs that are nearly adults are called froglets.

To become frogs, tadpoles go through a huge change. This change is called metamorphosis (say: met-ah-MORF-ah-siss). At around 5 weeks a tadpole will grow tiny legs. By around 14 weeks it has grown **lungs** and looks more like an adult frog.

Insects

Like frogs, some insects go through metamorphosis too. Some young insects will look completely different to their parents. For example, dragonflies start life as **nymphs** that live underwater.

Dragonfly nymphs don't have wings and look rather different from their parents.

When they are ready to go through metamorphosis, the nymphs come to the surface of the water. After climbing onto a reed or plant, they will then moult. The adult dragonfly will crawl out of its old skin.

Plants

Plants start their lives as seeds, which are made by adult plants. Seeds take in lots of water from the ground until they burst. Then, a root will begin to grow downwards into the soil. Roots hold the plant in the ground and take in water and nutrients.

Shoot

Root

After the root, a shoot will begin to grow. A shoot grows upwards out of the soil while the root grows downwards. As a plant gets older, the shoot will become taller and will turn into a stem with leaves.

Why not plant a plant and watch it grow?

Humans

Human babies are very small when they are born, but they grow very fast. Human babies' heads are large compared to their bodies. Children's bodies grow faster than their heads for the first few years of their lives.

As humans get older, growth slows down.

Humans grow and change quickly around the ages of 11 to 17. This is called puberty. It is when children's bodies become more like adult bodies. At around 18 years old, humans stop growing taller.

Glossary

gills	the organs that some animals use to breathe underwater
larvae	a type of young insect or fish that must grow and change before it can reach its adult form
lungs	bag-like organs that some animals use to breathe
nutrients	natural substances that plants and animals need to grow and stay healthy
nymphs	the young of some insects that go through metamorphosis
processes	a series of activities or natural changes
young	an animal's offspring or babies

Index